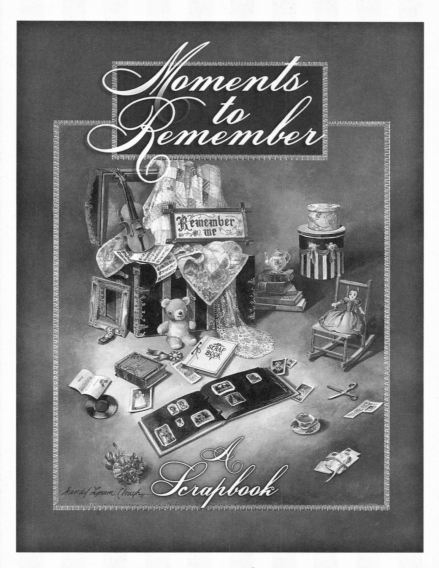

Paintings by
SANDY LYNAM CLOUGH

HARVEST HOUSE PUBLISHERS
Eugene, Oregon

Memories of

_____

Happy times and bygone days are never lost....

In truth, they grow more wonderful within the heart that keeps them.

KAY ANDREW

May you always have pleasant memories of us...

THE BOOK OF
1 THESSALONIANS

I am with you,

Wandering through memory lane.

B.G. DeSylva

The heart holds, like remembered music, a landscape grown too dark to see.

GWEN HARWOOD

Back on its golden wings,

The gate of Memory swings,

And my heart goes into the garden

And walks with the olden things.

ELLA WHEELER WILCOX

I am thankful for every remembrance of you...

THE BOOK OF PHILIPPIANS

Memory is not just the imprint of the past upon us;

it is the keeper of what is meaningful for our deepest hopes....

ROLLO MAY

In memory everything seems to happen to music.

TENNESSEE WILLIAMS

We must always have old memories, and young hopes.

ARSENE HOUSSAYE

Memory is a child walking along the seashore.
You never can tell what small pebble it will pick up and
store away among its treasured things.

PIERCE HARRIS

The experiences you have had are your own greatest treasure,
well worth the remembering and retelling.

RAY MUNGO

The memory of the righteous will be a blessing…
THE BOOK OF PROVERBS

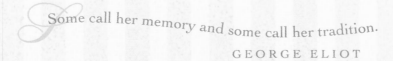
Some call her memory and some call her tradition.

GEORGE ELIOT

The more you love a memory, the stronger and stranger it is.

VLADIMIR NABOKOV

We do not remember days,
we remember moments.

CESARE PAVESE

According to your love, remember me...

THE BOOK OF PSALMS

Memory is the only way home.

TERRY TEMPEST WILLIAMS

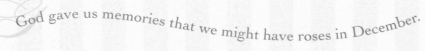

God gave us memories that we might have roses in December.

JAMES M. BARRIE

The heart has its own memory, like the mind,

and in it are enshrined precious keepsakes,

into which is wrought the giver's loving touch.

HENRY WADSWORTH LONGFELLOW